PHILOSOPHY IN DON QUIXOTE: COMMENTARY ON THE MEDITATIONS OF ORTEGA Y GASSET

by Oswald Sobrino

Dedicated to my father, Osvaldo Sobrino y Laffont (1937-1994), who first introduced me to the works of José Ortega y Gasset

CONTENTS

◆◆◆

INTRODUCTION

In 1914, the very young José Ortega y Gasset (he would die about 40 years later in 1955) wrote his first book, *Meditations on Quixote (Meditaciones del Quijote).* During those 40 years, he would become a one-man revival of philosophy in Spain. What an apt beginning to the revival of a serious and accessible way of doing philosophy in Spain, the only nation (I think) in which the national hero is a fictional character!

This small book (really what some would call a "digital pamphlet") follows my earlier book on Ortega and the idea of philosophy (*Freedom and Circumstance).* Since the book is part of a series, I make no apologies for its brevity, a brevity that is more common in book publishing today as exemplified by Oxford's "very short introductions" series and by Amazon's genre of short e-books. In this short book, I will go deeper, to the earliest roots of Ortega's revolutionary approach to philosophy--an approach in which the vital, life itself, takes precedence over our abstractions. The categories of life become the key to philosophy. Where did he get the inspiration for this "vital" philosophy? Let's find out. At the same time as I communicate what I find in Ortega, I will record my own reactions. To encounter Ortega is to philosophize. These pages will contain much of Ortega but also, inevitably, much of myself. As the ancients knew, to make a commentary, to reread a great author is to create anew. The pattern of these pages is simple: I describe what Ortega writes and then react. Compared to my earlier book on Ortega, this one has been more of a challenge. In the *Meditations*, we need to read even more between the lines to infer what the philosopher is telling us. The erudite commentary of Julían Marías is of enormous help in that reading between the lines. (The Marías commentary accompanies the Spanish edition of the *Meditations* that I have used.)

But why bother with Ortega? Ortega gives us clarity about living, about life. We are caught up in life. Clarity would be a nice thing to have. Fortunately, unlike many other philosophers, Ortega writes clearly. *Vamos sin miedo (Let's go forward without fear.)*

Note to the Reader: I will refer parenthetically to the pages of the edition of *Meditaciones del Quijote*, which I have carried for years in my library, an edition published in Spanish in 1957 as part of the Biblioteca de Cultura Básica, Ediciones de la Universidad de Puerto Rico, Revista de Occidente, Madrid. As noted before, the commentary of the great philosopher Julián Marías accompanies this edition.

I will identify the part of Ortega's book that I am writing about either as the title of my chapters, or parenthetically if I devise my own chapter title, so that the English-speaking reader can easily read the corresponding Ortega chapter in an English translation of his choice (the only English translation I am familiar with is the Norton Library Edition published in 1963, with an introduction by Julían Marías). For example, my Chapter 1 corresponds to Ortega's introduction to the reader labeled "Lector" (Reader) in Spanish. In contrast, Chapter 2's title is the same as the title used by Ortega for the first section of his book. I devise my own title for Ch. 3 covering the final section of Ortega's book. My own conclusion rounds off my treatment of Ortega's work. The Table of Contents provides an easy guide to what I have just described. As you can see, Ortega's book, like Gaul, is divided into three parts: his introduction to the reader (my Ch. 1), his preliminary meditation (my Ch. 2), and his meditation on the novel (my Ch. 3).

◆◆◆

CHAPTER 1: ORTEGA TO THE READER ("LECTOR")

Ortega´s introduction to his meditations is not what the typical reader assumes. Ortega´s prolegomenon is itself philosophical work essential to the entire book. In fact, Ortega´s most famous quotation ever lies in the introduction: "I am I and my circumstance: if I do not save it, I do not save myself" (43-44).

Our task is to see how his thread of reasoning leads to this famous assertion of an "I" that cannot be divorced from its circumstance. At the very beginning of his introduction, Ortega alerts the reader: I am going to think in reference to "Spanish circumstances" (13). The first impression is that this writer is confessing his parochialism. This understandable impression will gradually dissipate as we follow Ortega's "essay" (13).

First, Ortega examines his motive for writing: *amor intellectualis* or "intellectual love," that is, love for understanding (14). This love is aimed at the realities that life exposes as if they are remnants from a shipwreck (*naufragio*; 14). In his later writing, Ortega will develop the image of the shipwreck in describing the situation of each individual in the world. This motivating love seeks to understand what is presented in and to the life of the individual. The goal of this love, like that of all loves, is to seek the "perfection of the beloved" so that the beloved achieves her "plenitude" (15).

This love is quite egalitarian and democratic; it encompasses and embraces all things:

> Blessed be all things! Love them, love them! Each thing is a fairy that disguises with misery and vulgarity its interior treasures and is a virgin that must be seduced in order to make herself fertile. (15)

This attitude or perspective on reality, on things, on the *res,* is clearly mystical in nature. What we have is a rational mysticism which reacts deeply to things encountered with a passion to understand them profoundly and thus, so to speak, to "perfect" them. The opposite of this love is the hate that leaves us distant from things, closed to them, in a sad universe that is then "rigid, dry, sordid, and deserted" (17). Here we have Ortega the early 20th century phenomenologist who seeks the profound reality of things as we open ourselves to them in the experience of life. At this point, it is good to note that the word "perspective" is crucial for Ortega's thought. Already in his first book, Ortega emphasizes the teaching that the search for truth is self-consciously perspectival, a search very much aware that its circumstance is limited to a particular perspective (41-43). This awareness immunizes against fanaticism and opens us to the never-ending task of integrating new perspectives into those we already possess or with which we are already familiar. We do not fear the new.

What does this love do to the things it loves? It binds the beloved thing to oneself and to all other things. Ortega embraces the Platonic project of an *eros* seeking "that everything be joined to itself" (18). Ortega calls this passion for understanding an "erotic passion" (21). The ethics of passionately seeking to comprehend the other is for Ortega an "integral ethics" that is not distorted by a dogmatic and fixed ethics (26-27).

What Ortega thus proposes is "philosophy as the general science of love," a notion that is clearly Platonic in inspiration (28). At the same time, this notion of philosophy is very compatible with the Christian notion that the deity itself is love and that all things are created through this love (see especially 1 John 4:8, and the famous prologue to the Gospel of John). Love becomes the motor of the universe. Another very Christian trait of this Orteguian philosophy of love is its self-conscious, non-dogmatic, open stance of humility to the things of the world: "I offer only a *modi res considerandi* [a mode of considering things], potential new ways of looking at things" (33). These observations are humbly offered for testing by the reader to see if they are fruitful; the reader "will test their truth or error by means of his intimate and genuine experience" (33).

What then has Ortega given us thus far? He has proposed a philosophical approach that is non-pretentious because based on the motivations of a human being facing the world. The motivations are not bracketed and ignored. We do not jump into a deductive systematic philosophy. In true phenomenological fashion, we are first invited to define and describe our stance toward the world as individuals possessing a semi-mystical and passionate urge to fully understand the things in our world. There is no pretence here of some omniscient and dogmatic view that grasps the entire world's meaning at one leap, a view common to fanatics of all kinds, whether they are secular or religious. What we have instead is a very realistic description of the lover of wisdom, the philosopher, a human being with a passion to profoundly enter into the things he or she encounters in the world and seeking to share those experiences with others so that others may judge their authenticity. By the middle of the 20th century, this approach will be readily recognizable as both phenomenological and existentialist.

Of immense importance for the future philosophical work of Ortega over many coming decades is the emphatic embrace of the humble realities that surround us: "Circumstance! *Circumstantia!* The mute realities that are present in our closest surroundings!" (35). Why this emphasis on circumstance? Here again, we see the phenomenological, inductive turn: philosophy will not and should not begin as an abstract system but will be born from what we pay attention to in our surroundings. For Ortega, philosophy can be said to be paying attention to our situation, to our circumstance.

Interestingly, Ortega seeks to bring us to matters that we normally do not consider significant. He seeks to draw our attention to what lies under and through our preoccupation with politics and social issues. For example, Ortega calls attention to the cultivation of friendship, to the cultivation of joy in the realities around us (38). This care for the realities of our circumstance is to seek the *logos* of each reality: "the meaning, the nexus, the unity, all that is individual, immediate, and circumstantial, that appears to be merely casual or lacking in meaning" (39). The task of this new philosophical focus is to extract "the *logos* from a reality that was still viewed as insignificant (that is, 'illogical')" (40).

In the end, Ortega offers us a task: "the reabsorption of our circumstance is the concrete destiny of humanity" (43). In the end, each life has a calling, a *munus*, an *officium*, namely, to find the meaning of its circumstance. That process is the process of living authentically. At this point, Ortega reaches the affirmation that is the most quoted of his many quotable statements: " I am I and my circumstance, and if I do not save it, I do not save myself " (44). He even refers to the Bible by quoting this Latin aphorism: "Benefit that place in which you have been born" (*Benefac loco illi quo natus es*; 44). In Platonic terms, "save the appearances" (44). In other words, save the world since the world we experience is an experience of appearances whose *logos* or meaning must be uncovered.

This saving is thus the task of finding the meaning or *logos* of all that stands around us (44). The spirit that animates this vital task of discovering the meaning of our circumstance is optimistic. Ortega affirms that "there is nothing in the world through which a divine nerve does not pass through: the difficulty lies in reaching it and to make contact with it" (44). As a result, we are engaging in a form of heroism when we seek to save our circumstance--"the possibility of heroism exists everywhere hidden and each human being, if he strikes with vigor the ground where he stands, can expect to discover a spring" (45). As Ortega says, "For Moses the Hero, every rock is a spring" (45).

In the next few pages, Ortega gives us a brief study of Spanish reactionaries. For us, it would be better to focus on the more generic term for the phenomenon that Ortega analyzes: fanaticism, a problem common to all cultures, nations, and religions. Fanaticism murdered Jesus of Nazareth and keeps slaughtering many today. Ortega gives us a perspective on fanaticism that is of great value in its concise capturing of this dark reality. Ortega focuses on the key trait of all forms of fanaticism. The fanatic ("reactionary") is unable "to treat the past as a way of life. . . . [and instead] rips it from the sphere of the living and enthrones it, thoroughly dead, to rule over humanity" (50). Ortega calls this key trait of fanaticism the "inability to keep the past as something living" (50).

We see fanaticism in forms of religious fundamentalism. The forms and even language of a particular era are imposed on the present in a way that the people of that era would not recognize. For example, the Latin of the Vulgate which was intended to make the Bible accessible to the masses becomes the means to make religion unintelligible to the masses in the present. In politics, the forms and rhetoric of a simpler agricultural society are imposed on a post-industrial present of powerful corporations. The fanatic claims to celebrate forms that have been deprived of their reason for being and so the forms themselves become targets of disdain.

The self-consciously non-fanatical stance of Ortega is crucial in an era in which individuals read only the media that matches their ideological taste and seek to interact only with those who already agree with them. That is why you will often see in daily life the shock that arises when a closeted ideologue meets someone who not only disagrees but disagrees in a disconcertingly assertive and intelligent way. The cloistered ideologue has never had such an encounter and so often falls to pieces as the ground shakes under his feet. The messenger of such a shock is often made the scapegoat for the fanatic's unpleasant sensations of vertigo. Socrates told us that the unexamined life is not worth living. The fanatic, who, *ipso facto*, has not examined himself, is not worth debating.

The non-fanatical alternative recommended by Ortega is quite appealing: "Every day I am less interested in judging, of being the judge of things, I begin [instead] to prefer being the lover of things" (52). Ortega applies this reverence for things to the task of the literary critic whose task is "to complete the work . . . . [so that] the average reader may receive as intense and clear an impression of a particular work as possible" (52; emphasis added). This completing of the work is an act of charity, of *agape.* We perform it for the work and so also for the author and the audience. This advice is Ortega's evangelical counsel to the intellectual.

In applying this counsel to complete *Don Quixote,* Ortega urges us not to focus so much on the character named "Don Quixote" as on Cervantes the author of the novel who created the character. By focusing on Cervantes, we can uncover the message of a work that is neither simplistic nor merely romantic nor merely comic. We can, in this way, avoid the superficial "dualism" of either rejecting a crazed Don Quixote or of embracing an absurd Don Quixote appropriate to an allegedly absurd world (55). Thus, for Ortega, to meditate on the novel is to meditate on Cervantes the author present in this particular work (56).

How then should the literary critic proceed? Not with a frontal brutal assault. Rather, the critic proceeds to understand the novel in the same way that the ancient Hebrews captured Jericho beginning "with broad sweeps around the target, [as] our thoughts and emotions gradually narrow their focus," imitating the ancient trumpets that captured the Canaanite city (58). By making this reverential circling of the great novel, Ortega aims to redeem or save his particular circumstance in history: Spain (59). In our own very different circumstance, we can imitate the approach of Ortega by refusing to be reactionaries who lift up a dead past, or to be irrationalists who do not bother to pay close attention to our circumstance.

Tying It All Together

What then can we conclude from Ortega's "Note to the Reader"?

1. Love or *eros* impels us to understand our shipwrecked condition: our circumstance arouses our desire to understand.
2. Our knowing is based on our own perspective, a fact that precludes the fanaticism that rejects the perspectives of others.
3. The goal of this "erotic" knowing is to uncover the *logos* or meaning of things, even the most humble and usually unnoticed things.
4. Intellectual work is an act of charity or *agape*, which seeks to uncover the treasures of a novel or other work of art for others.
5. The process of understanding things takes the form of a respectful and repetitive circling of the thing; it does not take the form of a brutal, frontal assault. So much for the polemics favored by political and religious fanatics.

◆ ◆ ◆

CHAPTER 2: PRELIMINARY MEDITATION

Ortega begins his preliminary meditation by focusing on a particular setting: the monastery-palace of El Escorial outside Madrid, built by Philip II of Spain in the 16th century (67-68). The site is almost alpine in its feel, with austere architecture that is far from the stereotypical view of Spain as the land of flamenco dancers and fiestas. You find here the stoicism of Castile and its sober grandeur. Ortega sets this location as the *mise en scene* of his meditations and describes with voluptuous detail the fauna, the trees, the flowers that he finds striking.

Ortega's beginning *in medias res* ("in the middle of things") is true to his philosophy: I am I and my circumstance. I cannot explain my life without first paying close attention to what surrounds me. The universal is found in caring about the particular. This particular Spaniard begins in Castile. A person from another nation or from another region of Spain would begin somewhere else. Ortega's philosophical message is one of mindful presence: be attentive (as some Eastern Christian liturgies like to repeat and as Buddhism also recommends). Be attentive to where you go and where you are. The boundaries between the ego, the I, and circumstance are hazy: the "I" cannot find itself apart from the circumstance. This approach is in sharp dissent from our habitual individualism, especially strong in the United States, in which we act like monads isolated from our setting. *We do not begin with a monad: we begin immersed in a particular circumstance that breathes centuries of history and interpretation.*

We have, for example, the experience of rediscovering ourselves by means of our circumstance when we revisit the places of our youth. We return with nostalgia to rediscover ourselves in an old chapel, an old school, an old street, an old neighborhood, an old house or apartment building. These places make up our ego: they carry meaning that allows us to engage in self-discovery, to recover who we are. As we move forward in life, we forget so much of ourselves. We have to return to certain settings, either literally or in our thoughts, to rediscover and renew all the dimensions of our self. The places carry us within their walls and in their streets. Reality is impregnated with the self because the places have been inhabited by us. They have shaped us. Pope Francis has eloquently spoken of nostalgia, the yearning to return, in the context of immigration. We also sense that yearning, not a yearning necessarily to reverse our migration, but to revisit the places that can reveal us once again to ourselves and thus renew our identity with a new profundity. Thus, one of the best things anyone can do is to take a pilgrimage back to his past as a way to know how to face the future. (But if the past was full of dysfunctional people, the pilgrim may need to be very cautious and maintain a careful physical distance.)

A. The Forest

Ortega then proceeds to the first of fifteen sub-meditations within this preliminary meditation. The first one of these focuses on the idea of a forest. What Ortega proposes is that we never really see the forest--we see trees from the forest, but the forest itself remains an idea: "the sum of our possible actions that upon being realized lose their authentic value" (71). The sensation is of reality as something fleeting that eludes us and inspires a certain awe and mystery. We find here a strain of contemplative mysticism appropriate to the land that gave us the great mystics Teresa of Jesus and John of the Cross.

B. Depth and Surface

Ortega then gives us a marvelously subtle mediation on the mutual dependency of depth and surface and on the inanity of those wishing to recognize nothing beyond laser-like clarity. The ramifications here are manifold: the need to preserve individual privacy and to respect and to recognize the inevitability of mystery and of limits to our knowledge. These requirements further distance us from the ideologue and the fanatic.

He returns to the idea of the forest by analyzing this phrase: "the trees do not allow us to see the forest" (69). In the English idiom, we speak of "not seeing the forest for the trees." Ortega makes the point that it is precisely because of the trees that we know in the first place that a forest exists (72). The forest is obscured by the trees because the forest is that which lies hidden behind the trees. The reality of the forest is precisely a reality that is hidden or latent.

Ortega even gives a homely example: the struggling student who calmly accepts his place as last in the class and recognizes that someone must be last in order for anyone to be first (72). He makes the point that depth requires a hiding place, requires being last (73). At this point, Ortega makes a moral judgment that is crucial for dethroning the fanatic, the pushy, the busybody, the nag that we all know all too well:

> To ignore that each thing has its own condition and not that condition which we wish to demand of it is, in my view, the true capital sin, a sin which I call the "polite sin" because it originates in

> a lack of love. There is nothing more impermissible than to shrink the world with our obsessions and blindspots, to diminish reality, to suppress aspects of reality. . . . [T]here are things that show only what is strictly necessary so that we may discover them hidden behind the apparent (73).

What are some of the consequences from this insight? We respect the privacy of the other and discover what is hidden by means of that respect. The intimate needs to hide behind the surface in order to remain intimate in character. The often-mocked traditional view of modesty is a prime example, even if current society, obsessed with exhibitionism, is too obtuse to understand it.

From the point of view of the suitor, the woman worth pursuing is the one who preserves a hidden intimacy that is not flaunted superficially. She invites one to discover what is worth discovering because it lies deeply within her and not on the surface. This romantic example applies to all other forms of friendship. The exhibitionist depreciates himself by putting all his wares on view. Our social media makes this exhibitionism endemic and so diminishes friendship as an invitation to discovery.

In sexual behavior in which nothing is held in reserve, we find the shrinking of the person. Nothing is left to give because all has been given. We cheapen ourselves in the process. You do not need to be religious at all to see this pernicious dynamic: what must remain hidden is pushed forward so that it shrivels in the glare of its very promiscuity. The profound then becomes superficial and can no longer fulfill the task of the profound: to satisfy our deepest yearnings. In this type of cultural dynamic, the high rate of unhappy marriages and divorces is unsurprising. What is surprising is that anyone still bothers to get married at all in the first place. A culture of exhibitionism is a culture of disenchantment and disillusion. The result is a lack of joy and an increase in depressed personalities who find reality dispiriting even at a very young age.

Ortega refers to the profound as the "third dimension" (74). All love--and friendship is a form of love--involves discovering that third dimension. For Ortega, the proper response to reality is to love it, not to measure it. We save the phenomena (compare p. 44) by respectfully looking for that third dimension in all things and all persons that lies below the surface. A world where mystery has been vanished is a world that loses its charm. You can see this daily reality in any Western society and even beyond.

Ortega finds this truth self-evident in the commonplace. Looking even at an orange means that the other side of the orange is always hidden from us. Here lies the seed of the perspectivism for which Ortega would become famous in his later writings. We know by means of perspective; and, being consciously aware of that process, we learn subtlety and restraint in our pronouncements and are eager to discover the perspectives of others through conversation, dialogue, and listening.

For the literary critic or for any other reader, these insights mean that we do read between the lines and seek the truth in the silences of the text and search for the distant horizon that becomes a hermeneutical key for a text. To reduce reading or literary study to the mere rote recital of a list of characters, episodes, and plots is to miss the most important task of the reader: to find the interpretive key that reveals the meaning of the surface characteristics of the text found in these characters, episodes, and plots. In biblical studies, for example, all too often students are subjected to an informational avalanche of data (often tenuous and speculative, at that), instead of being invited to apply an interpretive key that can enlighten the details. We see the same lost opportunity in other fields dedicated to textual study: we become lost in the details instead of seeking to "save" the details. Classical philology has often descended to this lost opportunity of saving the text by failing to seek the depth lying below and behind the surface. Often, I suspect the scholar simply lacks the imagination, the vision, and magnanimity to pursue the profound and so permanently immerses himself in the comfortably trivial.

Turning to our fellow human beings, we can view each person as a living text, a story and a drama, inviting discovery. Written texts in fact are written most passionately for the purpose of discovery the reality of the persons appearing as its characters (*personae*). The ancient actors with masks are the *personae* whose masks we seek to remove. As many have observed, from Augustus to Shakespeare, life is like a play or drama. In this way, life is like a literary text; and every literary text is like life. We are searching for the depth of the human person before us and indirectly for our own depth as persons.

In searching for that depth, we as subjects must act. Otherwise, as Ortega notes, all we have are a series of present impressions. We impose varieties of distance on those impressions: some immediate, some farther along (79). Depth "requires more from us" (79).This requirement for more gives us the insight that profound realities reveal themselves only to those who "wish their existence" (81). We "push ourselves toward them"; these depths "exist only for those who have the desire for them" (79).

At this point, we can anticipate Ortega's famous distinction between the mass mentality and the mentality that seeks excellence (the "noble" mentality). The mass mentality is not curious for depth. It is happy to float haphazardly. The mentality seeking excellence pushes further. As Ortega points out in his later writings, this mass versus noble distinction is not necessarily one between the uneducated and the educated. Many a degree holder lives a mass mentality of superficiality on a daily basis. They are satisfied to examine life on the basis of banal cliches and slogans that are fashionable in their social circles.

This looking with greater depth at reality is the gaze that Plato ranked above mere looking (82). This active vision or viewing is "an idea" (82). When we actively gaze at the depth of things, we use "perspective" based on a "purely intellectual act" (83). Ortega will develop in his future writings this epistemology of perspectivism. Here we find the beginning of that future work. He gives the example of perceiving a worn-out color: we actively and immediately compare the full deep color of the fabric with its now faded condition (82-83).

C. An Age of Mediocrity

In the fifth section of his preliminary meditation, Ortega fiercely disdains the period of Spanish history called the Restoration (1874-1898), in which the monarchy was restored after the First Spanish Republic. This period ended with what the Spaniards call "the disaster," the loss of Spain's last colonies, Cuba, Puerto Rico, Guam, and the Philippines, to the rising United States as a world power. Ortega characterizes this period as one of mediocrity.

For Ortega, mediocrity is a way of living that in fact is a "not-living." For those familiar with existentialism, we can view mediocrity as a false consciousness that is the opposite of authentic life. And that is what mediocrity means in Ortega as exemplified during the Restoration when "fatally, the mediocre and the superficial appeared to increase in density" (87). Critics celebrated the mediocre because they had no experience of the profound (Id.). It was an age in which "places were occupied automatically by things and people continually becoming less suited to them" (86).

For Ortega, such an age of mediocrity could not read Cervantes with any profundity: "Just as there is a seeing which is a genuine gaze so there is a reading which is an understanding ("*intellegere*") or a reading of what lies inside, a thoughtful reading" (89). That lack of thoughtful reading made it impossible to understand the

Quixote (89).

Can this analysis of literary criticism help us in reading our lives intelligently? It is an analysis that cautions us to beware the applause of the experts who can applaud the mediocre when they lack the vision to see the profundity of life.

One of the great frustrations of life is the reality that what appears wise or expert or intelligent often is none of these at all. Social and intellectual elites are often at the service of mediocrity. Yet, that mediocrity is very well disguised by the social prestige of the elite. We think that *they* must know something we do not know in order to claim to see value in what seems merely mediocre. Ironically, Ortega, whose philosophy has a strain of elitism, is cautioning us to beware mediocre elite opinion that can thoroughly dominate an entire historical period--a mediocre period in which we do not really live but only dream of living (85). The great leaders and celebrities of the age are not really great--they are only what they imagine themselves to be (85-86). Social status and prestige make the mediocre appear great with the result that mediocrity ends up defining greatness itself.

The mediocre is the inauthentic, and intellectuals as masters of abstractions are the foremost in promoting the inauthentic. The authentic intellectual pursues a profound looking at the concrete reality around him or her. That vocation is a calling to be genuine, something which phenomenology will attempt in philosophy: to return to the things themselves, to penetrate experience rather than to make it bloodless. In our own lives, we must ask ourselves if we are able to put aside the spectacles of conscious and unconscious ideology that falsify reality and to look with fresh, unobstructed eyes at concrete things and concrete actions. Often, the result of really looking again at reality is a completer reversal of our previous beliefs and assumptions. That “taking off” of our spectacles is the task of the intellectual for himself and for others.

D. The Delusion of Ethnocentrism

Ortega begins this chapter in a way that will seem dated to us in the 21st century. He begins talking about how as a youth he had read about "Latin clarity" (as in the clarity of Italians, Spaniards, and Frenchmen) and "Germanic cloudiness" (90-91). Then, he practices what he preaches in this section: meditation as a profound gaze to uncover the depth of things and ideas, a meditation that requires effort and struggle to accomplish (90).

What Ortega concludes is that his youthful reading had mislead him. Instead of a simplistic contrast between Germanic and Latin, Ortega concludes that the crucial concept is not the misleading one of a "Latin culture," but rather the more fruitful idea of a Mediterranean culture (93). The precise reasoning that leads Ortega to this specific resolution is not crucial for our purposes. What is crucial is that the thinker struggles and wrestles with oversimplistic concepts until he or she finds a more adequate one, more adequate because it is more realistic and less misleading, although we will never attain the perfect concept that cannot be improved in some way. New generations and thinkers will keep pushing forward.

Too often, in social life, we allow ourselves to be imprisoned by the reigning, unquestioned ideas in our environment. The thinker is not satisfied with confused ideas, however regnant and dominating. The thinker pushes forward. The lesson for us is to distrust musty concepts that persist because no one questions them. The issue of race or ethnicity is one of these concepts. Even today, many attribute some mysterious force or power to their own ethnicity, which, of course, being their own, is in some way superior to other ethnicities. The more enlightened view relativizes all ethnicities: we share one human nature that facilitates profound communion and communication between individuals of the most diverse and exotic backgrounds. That reality is why a 21st century American or African or native of China can be deeply moved by a 19th century Russian novel. That primary reality of a common human nature keeps our silly and vain ethnocentric tendencies in check. An old saying has it that patriotism is the last refuge of a scoundrel. We can add "nationalism" and "ethnocentrism" to the list. Like Ortega, we need to gaze more profoundly at reality in order to liberate ourselves from juvenile confusions. It is good for a young person to develop a healthy pride in his cultural background--but if he needs to keep going back frequently to that well to achieve a sense of security or identity, then he has got problems; and so will those around him who often will not even share the same cultural identity.

E. A Critique of Sensuality

Ortega continues his pursuit of what is distinctively Latin or, more correctly, Mediterranean with a critique of sensuality (100). The upshot of his meditation on sensuality is that it poses a danger, a danger in which we can lose ourselves. He compares sensuality to the violent attack of a wild animal, a panther, which grabs us through the senses and not the intellect. The danger is thus that "this invasion . . . may dislodge us from ourselves, empty out our intimacy, and . . . leave us transformed into post gates on the highway through which comes and goes the chaotic mass of things" (106).

That is a critique we need to hear, especially in an age when our exposure to the chaotic mass of things has been exponentially multiplied by the Internet and its images. The question to ask ourselves is whether we have become mere consumers, or whether we are also producers who shape our circumstance. Here is a direct link to Ortega's famous dictum that "I am I and my circumstance." Do I affect my circumstance, or am I only acted upon by my circumstance? In other words, if it is only a matter of circumstance, then the "I" disappears so that, in contrast to Ortega's dictum, then the person lost in sensuality can say only "I am my circumstance," with the "I" gone. That is the risk of being a mere receptacle for sensual bombardment. We can do better.

F. Eros as the Engine for Understanding the Other

This critique of sensuality is followed by what may, at first, seem a contradiction: love or eros is the engine of seeking the profound meaning (*sentido*) of the other (110-111). That meaning of the other lies in a structure which is the web of relations of a thing so that the thing becomes, so to speak, the center of its universe (108,110). Again, recall Ortega's "I am I and my circumstance"--in other words, I am I and my relations to others. This fundamental social reality is why American libertarianism with its exaggerated isolationist individualism is so trivial a proposition to anyone who thinks deeply about the human person.

Ortega waxes poetic in his original Spanish when agreeing with Plato that eros is the urge to understand:

> Plato sees in "eros" the impetus that leads us to link things among themselves; it is--he says--a unitive force and the passion for synthesis. For this reason, in his view, philosophy, which seeks the meaning of things, is induced by "eros." Meditation is an erotic exercise. The concept is an amorous ritual .... perhaps, Nietzsche is right when he exclaims: Live dangerously! (111, my translation)

Ortega here captures the experience of the passionate thinker who is moved by the desire to possess the meaning, the profundity, of the other.

G. Concepts Are Not Killers of Life

In a beautiful series of paragraphs, Ortega then makes the case for the rational without falling into the trap of excessive rationalism. This meditation focuses on the "concept." First, he makes clear that his starting-point is quite different from the usual reflex of making the rational replace the vital emotions of lived experience. Ortega asserts that reason "cannot, [and] does not need to aspire to substitute for life" (114). Such a possibility is absurd given that reason itself is "a vital and spontaneous function tracing itself to the same origin as the senses of seeing and touching" (114).

Here is the "vitalism" or philosophy of life of Ortega: instead of the Cartesian "I think therefore I am," Ortega asserts "I live therefore I think."

Reason is a vital necessity and function because, as Plato noted, "impressions escape us if we do not weave them together by means of reason" (115). Hence, the "concept" is crucial as "the form, the physical and moral meaning of things" (115). We cannot reduce life to reason, but we cannot fully grasp life without reason: "Not everything is thought, but without thought we cannot fully possess anything" (116). Thus, each concept "is literally an organ by which we seize upon things" (116).

This vital view of the role of reason transcends the false conflict between emotions and sensuality and reason. Reason becomes a pragmatic tool for further embracing the fullness of life itself. As others have observed before me, Ortega's own brand of existentialism is thus far removed from any form of fashionable irrationalism or deconstructionism. Rather, reason is revered because it is essential to living.

The vital function of reason and its concepts is to secure life. As the old saying goes, thinkers build on the shoulders of giants who preceded them. Ortega refers to the "tranquil, definitive embrace of the achievements of others" (117). In contrast, in a critique of Spanish culture, Ortega singles out an "impressionistic culture" in which the thinkers and artists act like "Adams" who are reinventing the wheel at every turn (117). Ortega links this "Adam" complex to the frontier nature of Spanish culture seeking to reconquer its lands. In contrast, the Greeks give us the concept "not to substitute for spontaneity but rather to secure it" (119). The "Adam" complex is thus one of foolish arrogance. I start all over without bothering to submit myself and my thoughts to the best that has surely preceded me. Later in his life, Ortega will speak of the mentality of the "mass man" who does precisely this: he opines without bothering to consult the works of others before him. He fancies himself self-sufficient in his own arrogance, an arrogance that is present among both the uneducated and the highly educated.

H. The Concept is the Problem Solver

For Ortega and for us, life is problematic. The concept is the way we seek solutions (124). Interestingly, Ortega makes clear that an "idea" for Plato is "a point of view" (124). Here we see the origins of Ortega's later development of perspectivism. What is most interesting in this small section of his book is his abrupt declaration of the mission of a human being: "the mission of the human being on earth is clarity" (123). That mission lies deep within the human being and is "the root of his constitution" (122).

What better reason for becoming educated? What better reason for learning how to write clearly? What better reason for learning the grammar that enables us to write and think clearly? Unfortunately, most human beings begin, live, and die confused. Their thoughts are confused, their words are confused, their sentences (or attempted sentences) are confused.

This confusion does not keep individuals from being dogmatic and fanatical and from uttering absurdity blithely in order to contradict and engage in polemics. The polemical individual is the most mediocre of individuals. For him, the priority is winning and attacking, not gaining clarity. As we would say today, we are "wired" for clarity; yet, everywhere, we are confused (recall the parallel saying of Marx that man was born free but is everywhere in chains).

Ideology is the great haven for confusion. Ideology creates ready-made answers that solve none of the problematic aspects of life. Ideology itself becomes another problem, a problem that imposes itself imperially on all of life's facts by trying to freeze the evolving facts of life. For this reason, ideology is the anti-vocation of the human mind whose real vocation is clarity. Yet, most conflicts are based on ideology; and so, unsurprisingly, they rarely solve any problems.

The ideologue, the pharisee, the fanatical right-winger, the fanatical left-winger will not solve problems, but rather prolong them or multiply them. The man or woman who dares to step out of ideology--who is secure enough to do so, a security that is all too rare--will give us clarity. The ideologue will serve only his own desires, ambitions, and delusions. Ortega seeks for Spain a step beyond mere sensual impressions. He issues a call for an integration that "affirms and organizes its sensuality by cultivating meditation" (127). Ideology cultivates the raw desire for self-aggrandizement. In contrast, art--whether involving paintings or sculpture or music or literature--seeks to reflect on and ponder desires.

Ortega offers a small parable recounting an incident involving the North Pole explorer Parry who spent an entire day heading north, only to discover later that he had ended up further south because he had been traveling on a huge block of ice that was being dragged south by the ocean currents (130). Many of us, like Parry, think we are advancing toward a goal when in fact the advance is illusory. Instead, we are being dragged further and further away from the goal. This parable illustrates the deception from living life based on mere impressions concerning our progress.

I. Look for Contradictions

In this section, Ortega begins by commanding that any thinker worth her salt should begin by looking for contradictions in any reality because "what makes a problem a problem is its containing a real contradiction" (130). Too often we fail to look for contradictions. We are satisfied with the superficial when it comes to individuals and, as Ortega emphasizes, even when it comes to entire cultures. For example, my own hometown of New Orleans, a place I have deep affection for, is full of contradictions. We claim to "let the good times roll" and to have a great "joie de vivre"; but, in fact, the specter of violent crime and shameful poverty lurks all around the city. How can that specter be part of the "good times"? In addition, much of the "good times" is tied to gluttony and alcohol abuse, which make for very bad times in short order. A person *thinking* about the culture of New Orleans would carefully consider these contradictions and not be satisfied with tourist propaganda. (A similar dynamic is at work in many other cultures. For example, we can cite the alcohol abuse and other forms of abuse in Irish Catholic culture, and the failure of Latin cultures to come to grips with the high costs of political corruption that undermine societies from Latin America to Italy. In the United States, we have the contradiction of pursuing happiness by the ever more stressful and dehumanizing accumulation of consumer goods ostentatiously displayed.)

In Ortega's particular historical circumstance, the thinker will focus on the contradictions of Spanish culture; but the lessons are clearly applicable to our own different cultural circumstance. Ortega makes clear that entire cultures can profoundly fail in significant ways. Deviation from the originally vibrant and healthy impulses of a particular culture results in "failed products which are ineffective and insufficient," so that with each passing day a particular "people becomes less than what it should have been" (132).

For Spain (and other wounded cultures) to find renewal, Ortega calls for the thinker "to go against tradition and beyond tradition" (133). Here "tradition" means for Ortega the falsification of the true potential of a culture wrapped in harmful stereotypes. Ortega seeks the solutions to a failed tradition in a culture's healthy achievements. As to Spain, the work and style of Cervantes is one of those privileged cultural monuments where renewal can be found.

Tying It All Together

We have methodically reviewed what Ortega wrote in his "Preliminary Meditation" in his first published book dating to 1914. What can we conclude?

1. We are not isolated, individual monads but are rather social beings immersed in our circumstance. We find ourselves by embracing our circumstance.
2. To love or befriend another person and to uncover the reality of our circumstance require respect and reverence for the hidden, the private, the latent. Exhibitionism derails the process of understanding the profundity of persons and of our world.
3. We also have to beware of mediocrity and know that it can be socially celebrated as if it were not in fact mediocrity but its opposite. Our circumstance influences our view of reality. If society is mediocre, then we will easily applaud the mediocre. The opposite of mediocrity is profundity, the gaze into the depth of realities.
4. The task of the thinker also includes revising and overthrowing unquestioned concepts and ideas that cloud reality. Ethnocentrism and nationalism are prime examples.
5. The exaggerated sensuality in which the person surrenders to his circumstance without engaging his intellect is a great danger. We see the danger in the dissipation and mindless hedonism of many social settings.
6. Eros, in contrast to sensuality, seeks to see things in a web of relations. Eros is an exercise in understanding, while mere sensuality is pure reception.
7. The concept of reason is the *logos* or meaning of things.

Reason in the form of the concept is not anti-life but is what enables us to fully grasp life. Ortega rejects irrationalism.

8. Thus, a concept enables us to solve the problems of life by shedding clarity on them. In contrast, ideology imposes answers on life that do not address the ever-changing problems of life.

9. The thinker identifies the problems of life by not shying away from exposing the contradictions in lived reality, whether in societies, cultures, religions, or even households.

◆◆◆

CHAPTER 3: MEDITATION ON THE NOVEL ("FIRST MEDITATION")

Now, Ortega begins in earnest to focus on Cervantes' masterpiece. He begins by raising the issue of literary genre. He identifies Don Quixote as "the first novel both in terms of chronology and worth" (139). Ortega then seeks to meditate on the definition of a novel and begins by identifying the meaning of a literary genre.

In contrast to the classical view of genre as a fixed and abstract poetic form imposed on various types of poetry, whether epic or elegiac or lyric, Ortega views genres as "authentic aesthetic categories" (141), with each category presenting a fundamental theme in its most developed form. Thus, for Ortega, content and form are inseparable (141).

But what is the content of each genre? The genre's content is a fundamental and cardinal perspective on the human condition

(142). Again, we see the perspectivism of Ortega in its germinal form. He writes that: "each epoch brings with it a radical interpretation of the human. Better said, each epoch does not bring along such an interpretation but rather is that very interpretation. For this reason, each epoch prefers a particular genre" (142).

With Cervantes, the modern era, the era that prefers the novel as genre, unequivocally begins. We use the term "post-modern" to refer to contemporary culture, but we still prefer the "modern" novel as the queen of literary genres.

A. Ortega's History of Western Literature

Ortega then begins a lengthy search for the heart of the novel. He begins with the source of our Western literature, with Homer and the epic genre. His observations on epic are well worth the attention of any student of the classics. It is a shame that teachers of literature do not routinely quote Ortega's observations to students, whether in high school or college or graduate school.

Ortega asserts that the novel is the opposite of epic (148). In contrast to the accessible past of the novel, the past celebrated by epic is the archetypal, ideal past that we cannot identify as "our past" (149). This mythic past is in another dimension because it is incapable of aging (150). The mythic reflects cosmic forces that do not grow old (149). In a beautiful line, Ortega says that "Achilles is in fact as distant from Plato as he is from us" (150). In other words, even Plato was as detached from the mythic past of epic as we are today.

Thus, the form of the epic genre is archaic (151). The epic poet, like a prophet, does not invent anything but, rather, communicates what is immemorial and given (153-54). Unlike the novelist, the one who sings the epic is proudly unoriginal (153). The hexameter of the epic maintains this distance with its chanting and enchanting quality (156).

In sum, Ortega comes to three conclusions in his quest to define the novel:

1. The theme of the epic is the past as past, while the theme of the novel is that of current reality as current reality;

2. The characters of the epic are eternal and unique, while those of the novel are the typical ones we find in our streets and in our towns;

3. Art is a "technique, a mechanism for realization"; the poetic form is secondary (159). This realization articulates the theme of each epoch.

For students, these observations lead to deeper appreciation of the archaic, religious character of epic as a form of mythic prophecy, in contrast to the novel as the genre of our own times. Rarely do we find the difference articulated as forcefully and gracefully as done by Ortega in a few pages.

As Ortega continues his recapitulation of Western literary history, he next comes to mythology, which he defines as a revision of historical material that gives us the "Greek novel" (161). In light of *Don Quixote,* it is noteworthy that Ortega asserts that mythology has only one article of faith: "Adventure is allowed" (162).

B. The Books of Chivalry

Once science overthrows the reign of myth, we come to the works of adventure, that is, of chivalry (163). While these works of the imagination narrate the past, the novel, in contrast, describes things with which we are already familiar; chivalry, on the other hand, must create imaginary things that arouse our interest. The novel gives us things that we do not find interesting in themselves but presents and describes them in an interesting manner (164-65).

Chivalry, the literature of adventure, takes us from the world of reality to the world of the imagination, two worlds seen in Chapter 26 of *Don Quixote*, where Cervantes presents the comical scene of a puppet show that so overtakes the imagination of Don Quixote that Don Quixote actually enters the scene as a knight and puts an end to the puppet show (167ff.). In this episode, we see the two worlds in relation: reality and the imagination.

In this episode of the puppets, we see that a realist novel--a label we can apply to *Don Quixote* whose author seeks to attack tales of chivalry (170)--contains adventure within itself. The really existing character of Don Quixote in the novel wills and fantasizes about adventure and thus ironically puts adventure at the heart of the novel's realism (173).

C. Reality

With Cervantes, we enter the era of the Renaissance, we enter what philosophers call the "Modern World View," in which reality is what the laws of science describe and the rest is the subjectivity of the spectator, the human person (174). How then can the novel of Cervantes be a novel of adventure if it is anchored in the scientific realism of the Modern World View that arose with the Renaissance?

Cervantes in his realism will describe how the ideals of the subjective spectator arise. We see in Don Quixote the psychological process that gives rise to adventures, in contrast to myth which simply depicts the end result of adventure itself (177).

Ortega illustrates this psychological process that gives birth to adventures by focusing on the famous windmills of Don Quixote which, as all know, he viewed as giants. Ortega points out that we can't merely dismiss this episode as a product of the madness of Don Quixote for the simple reason that giants have never existed in reality; yet we humans have talked about giants since time immemorial (178). Like the mad knight, we have "seen" giants! Ortega proposes that the idea of giants is a reflection of some genuine reality, just as the windmills with their long arms lead to a vision of the arms of a giant (178). For Ortega, culture as the "ideal dimension of things" is thus not a world apart from earthly realities but is rather a reflection of those earthly realities (179).

Ortega then proceeds to define literary realism. He has already established that reality has an "ideal" aspect and a "material" aspect, as seen in the idea of a giant based on the material reality of a windmill (180). Realism is then emphasizing the purely material aspect of things (181). In the poetry of realism, we see the ideal, the mythical, as it descends into the purely material basis of reality (181). As he did previously, Ortega asserts that what moves us in the novel is not the reality but the representation of that reality (182).

So far, Ortega's analysis can leave the reader puzzled: where exactly does the charm of the novel's presentation lie?

Ortega answers in the next few pages: in the comic dimension. He tells us that reality acquires an "aesthetic interest" with the "comic intention" (184). Ortega also refers to this comedic aspect as "mime"--imitation for the sake of mockery ("burlarse"; 184). In conclusion, what is burlesque or mocking or ribald is the very texture of "all realism" and thus not an optional feature of the novel *Don Quixote* (184).

D. Hero and Heroism

Ortega is at his eloquent best in describing the hero and heroism (185). The subjective will to adventure that enters the reality of the novel and what makes adventure itself a reality is the heroic will. Here it is best to translate Ortega directly:

> [T]he will to adventure is real and true. . . . men exist committed to not being content with reality. They aspire that things take a different course, they refuse to repeat the gestures of custom and tradition . . . . We call these men heroes. Because to be

> a hero consists in being oneself, one's very self. If we resist the imposition by heredity and circumstance of certain actions, it is because we seek to locate in ourselves and only in ourselves the source of our actions. When the hero wills something, it is not his ancestors or present customs doing the willing but rather he himself is the one willing. This will to be oneself is heroism (186-187).

Ortega goes on to eloquently describe the life of the hero: "His life is a perpetual resistance to what is habitual and customary. Each one of his moves has had to first conquer custom and to invent a new way of acting. A life like that is perpetual suffering, a constant tearing out of that part of himself given over to habit and imprisoned by the material (187)."

E. Lyricism

This heroism is the "will to adventure" (187). Ortega cleverly illustrates the choice between the heroic and the non-heroic: either we embrace the heroic, or we easily resign ourselves to an unheroic reality in the same way that we wake up a person from his dreams (188). Ortega then turns to lyricism which he defines as poetry that expresses our human emotions and sentiments (188). Each era thus has its own lyricism because each era has its own subjective view of reality. Ortega, as I understand him, asserts that each era can take one of two views of heroism: the tragic view, which embraces heroism; and the comic view which shakes off the heroic as a serious proposition (190).

F. Tragedy and Comedy

For Ortega, the theme of tragedy is the will of the hero (191). When it comes to Greek tragedy, Ortega is pessimistic about our understanding it because of its roots in a religious context that we do not fully comprehend (191-92). Instead, Ortega focuses on the distinctive trait of tragedy as lying in the will of the hero to stubbornly engage in a superfluous adventure, an impulse alien to the prosaic mentality of those who seek to do only what is necessary (194).

Comedy, on the other hand, is the subversion of heroic tragedy. In comedy, the heroic will for adventure and for the ideal goes, as the proverb tells us, from the sublime to the ridiculous as the heroic will is overcome by reality (see 197, 199).

Ortega finally begins to bring us to a conclusion by labeling the novel as tragicomedy, the synthesis of tragedy and comedy (201). He looks to Plato as anticipating the novel when Socrates asserts that the same person is author of both tragedy and comedy (202).

G. The 19th Century

Ortega makes the major declaration that within every novel lies *Don Quixote* (203). Flaubert seems to agree when he touts the influence of Cervantes upon his work (203). Ortega neatly characterizes Madame Bovary reading her romantic novels as a Quixote in skirts (203). Yet, Ortega views the 19th century as a century of excessive realism that ends in bitterness (206). Darwinism sweeps out the heroic by putting each of us in a deterministic web (206-207) so that the novel aspires to be "physiology" (207). With this abrupt end, Ortega leaves us in limbo.

What can we infer from this abrupt ending? The 19th century has ended in a bitter, rancorous realism that excludes the heroic. As such, the great century of the novel has betrayed the Cervantine spirit which is stubbornly heroic because of the Knight's defining will to adventure. What comes next? Surely, renovation must lie, in Ortega's view, in a recovery of the Cervantine spirit of heroism which combines tragedy and comedy. As a result, the 19th century has fallen short of the greatness of Don Quixote; and renewal beckons so that we can once gain set forth on a heroic adventure that is both tragic and comic and preserves the free will of the hero and the *joie d'vivre* of his quest.

◆ ◆ ◆

CONCLUSION

The Meditations of Ortega are incomplete; they were never finished. Ortega abruptly stops his meditation with his description of *Don Quixote* as tragicomedy. As tragic, *Don Quixote* the novel contains the hero at its center with his will to adventure. As comedy, *Don Quixote* makes us laugh at the incongruity, the contrast, between the desire for high adventure and the stubborn reality of our prosaic, daily existence. The windmill is a monster, the shabby inn is a castle, the innkeeper can make one a knight, the poor working girls are ladies worthy of chivalry. We laugh at this comedy when we see our mistaken pretensions exposed. Yet, this comedy does not end with the merely absurd as in some forms of 20th century existentialism.

This tragic comedy teaches us that some degree of delusion is really an idealism and optimism that can transform reality into the adventure that the human spirit yearns for but which eludes us so often in the face of our disappointments. That healthy degree of delusion is a way to live heroically. For example, in some situations, people with some street smarts know that you must "act crazy" in order to defeat or neutralize the real crazies. We can extend that example to life as a whole. Is some degree of healthy delusion necessary for us to confront the disappointments of life that can easily crush our heroic spirit? Don Quixote the human being shows us a way to insert that idealism into the world so that we can transform the world a bit. We see an example of healthy delusion in the struggles of Franklin Delano Roosevelt with the crippling effects of polio on his legs. In spite of the lack of a cure, FDR maintained his outlook that the polio could be overcome and even ignored. That outlook led FDR to push forward to make history that rescued many from economic despair and from the enemies of freedom.

I am also reminded of a ninety-nine-year-old philosopher and social activist in Detroit, Michigan, who makes me smile because of her outrageous optimism in the midst of urban destruction and dysfunction. Her name is Grace Lee Boggs, a Chinese-American who was, surprisingly, part of the black civil rights movement in the United States. I picture her as an elderly woman, pushing a walker, in the devastated neighborhoods of Detroit; and I hear her say that she feels sorry for people who do not live in Detroit (see source below). I cannot avoid a smile, a smile suffused with admiration. Where others see only failure, she sees something from which to learn for the future, something that can be a lever for social and personal transformation. She is an example of a modern Don Quixote, whose optimism transforms his circumstance and the people whom he encounters. The characters of the novel begin to be infected with the knightly chivalry of Don Quixote, just as this elderly activist continues to infect people in Detroit with hope. [I highly recommend the documentary on Grace Lee Boggs, *American Revolutionary: The Evolution of Grace Lee Boggs* (2014), available at Amazon.com.]

Ortega has indeed left us enough of his meditations on the great novel of Cervantes to leave us, in my view, with this urgent proposal: Dare to bring the ideal, even with a dose of the ludicrous or even of delusion, to your circumstance in order to transform your circumstance and thereby yourself, given that, for each of us, "I am I and my circumstance."

◆ ◆ ◆

AUTHOR

Oswald Sobrino is a Ph.D. student in Latin and Roman Studies at the University of Florida. He has had a lifelong interest in Ortega's philosophy, which continues the search for wisdom and for understanding life that began in the West with the philosophers of the classical world.

www.ingramcontent.com/pod-product-compliance
Ingram Content Group UK Ltd.
Pitfield, Milton Keynes, MK11 3LW, UK
UKHW020137250726
13967UKWH00002B/708